On It Goes (Amidst the Chaos)

Tiàrnan McGarrity

Presentation by *BookLeaf Publishing*

Web: www.bookleafpub.com

E-mail: info@bookleafpub.com

ISBN: 9789358317237

First edition 2024

ACKNOWLEDGEMENT

I'd like to thank my parents, for their support, encouragement and belief.

Zara J, for being the most pure and kind hearted person that I've ever had the privilege to know.

Conor F, for listening to me go on and on and regularly checking in to see how things are going.

Will H, for being a prime example of how far a person can go, when they're willing to face the music and put in the work.

Bookleaf Publishing, for giving myself and many others this opportunity.

PREFACE

This moment has lasted years, stuck in a loop, the result dictating the action which dictates the result, which dictates the action and so on. The result came first. A thing already decided upon in the depths of the universal mind, it's decree carried out across the 10 Sephiroths, long before any action could take place. Yet the regret. What is its purpose? Is it simply a shackle? A means of control? Or perhaps it is a puzzle. A thing to be mused and mulled over again and again until the correct interpretation is stumbled upon. If this is the case, I've yet to come up with any correct answers. The whole thing's botched. Unless that's the point of all this. A living Kobiashi Mauru. That's an unwinnable situation to those not well versed in the world of Trek. Someone has to experience it. Given all the Worlds that live on this Earth alone, the spectrum of experience is a vast thing, and like any other spectrum, there are oddities, synchronisities, and those who are at the extremes.

After so long, that which stirs us, lays us to rest, that which engages us, turns away in apathy, that which embraces us, drops limp in the sun, and that which wounds us, acts as a salve, to stay the gushing flow, and urges us to make use of the dwindling time. Do something, before the clock ticks its last, before the lease on this matter runs out. Do not leave here in debt, do not live here in doubt. Help the other buddy out, lend them a hand, or an ear, or a fist, or whatever it is that they may need. There's much to be found in literature and music, in canvassed art or carved marble, or in the degree to which the human form can resemble such, after much discipline and effort; indeed, no less than life itself is to be found in such true expression, for it is ourselves, that gives life its meaning.

I've been entertained for too much of mine. I've spent more hours than I care to realise infront of a screen, watching, or gaming, or working. I've also spent more hours again doubting, replaying past failures, instances where, at the very crux, at the crucible, crucial point, the base program, having reached a critical stage of not being able to handle how well things are generally going and the possibilities of wonderment that could come, kicks in its failsafe, and brings all proceedings to a halt, usually with an asinine question, or a cold response, or even by complete ignorance. A subconscious set of laws that only allow for so much. It's quite the thing to watch yourself fuck things up over and over again in brand new, and disembowellingly, old, ways. It's been said before, more times than I care to count, but knowing is not 'half the battle'. It's the war council that's set up in preparation for the battle. It's the place where you choose a side, where previously held indoctrinations are thrown to the ever changing wind, it's the place where heroes are tainted and villains sanctified, if such things in their pure forms existed.

We all know they don't. We're all just people, hiding our warts and flashing our asses, just trying to get something, sometimes we don't even know what, and yet we all know people who would fit into either of these categories. I've seen and heard of many heroic deeds, but I'm better versed in the more villainous aspects of the human experience.

It's been a fateful year, I've tried to capture the essence of it in these pages, from snapshots of a moment, to more overarching narratives, trying to make sense out of it all, to carve out of a path of meaning. I hope at least some of it harmonises with you reader, not to wish ill-tidings upon anyone, but, life happens, and it's always good to know that we aren't alone when it does.

9 Haiku's

Sublime are the hills
On up from where few have gazed
It's time to move on

Memories can sting
Imaginations more so
Keep a level head

Those who can, must teach
Every lesson taught brings us
closer to ourselves

Every time we fail
we gain the experience
needed to succeed

Wondering out loud
risks great offence to those who
regrettably know

Even in the void
spontaneous things happen
Always expect change

Reality is

manifested by agreed
subconscious beliefs

Tenacity lies
in not listening to that
knowing little voice

Rest is essential
and the cornerstone of all
meaningful self worth

Fair Head

Salt strewn air brushes cracked lips
Late autumn sun flexes through light patterned
clouds
A studious ram studies warily from a steep
mound a-ways across the bog-patched and
tumultuous landscape
but soon goes back to its grazing

As the hill is crested, the heart drops
Jagged serenity juts out in a myriad of paths and
problems, before falling away sharply to certain
oblivion
where house to fist sized boulders scatter
downwards towards the quiet and expansive fury
of the ocean

Following the clifftop round to the east, a lake
exposes itself, feeding a perpetual glass stream
that spills down a steep gully
showing the way on down to the base
Care must be taken on the descent, as one slip
could prove fatal
Focus and physicality is demanded
and therein lies the steady thrill

The landscape of spattered rock and growth at
the bottom is harsh, unforgiving, and quick to
punish, yet also kind, understanding, and
timelessly patient, when respected
Gulls soar overhead, gliding above the clifftop
lip in relaxed daredevil circles

Scrambling among the dreadlocked spattering of
stone, all senses are required
There are cracks and holes and fissures and gaps
that drop down just deep enough for an ankle or
leg to be caught in, at best

Towards the rolling ocean, giant slabs of stone,
fallen from the cliff in bygone centuries, raise
the terrain in positive pitch northwards, at the
pinnacle of which, exudes a tall spire, aptly
named The Prow, just wide enough at the top to
sit upon

The pockmarked land, some 30ft below,
continues on only a short distance before
meeting the sea head on in its flirtations

There is no industry in such journeys, ones
position in the world will not change, there is
nothing to be gained materialistically

all that is to be found here, is a sense of peace,
universal perspective, and grateful unity, with
nothing other than the very land itself

Mute

Shamrock green and faded gold striped
wallpaper stares blankly
An old small ceramic table lamp cringes
The loose legged kitchen table starts to sweat
and the boy is mute

Sympathetic grey and sorrowful black
marshmallowed clouds leer
Castle-esq tower blocks loom ruinously
Cackling laughter reverberates
and the boy is mute

Sharp white flashes cut brightly across vision
and sense
Soft arms held limply
Virgin knuckles hang resigned to fate
and the boy is, still, mute

Scarlet red velvet curtains blush warmly
The laden bed flirtatious with intent
Suggestive words delight thoroughly
and the boy is, unbelievably, still, mute

Harsh yellow lines cruelly highlight fate
Unjustifiable logic dancing in victory

Faux-concern presented as ritual
and the boy, mute

Disappointedly stained blue skies hover
helplessly
Silent unseen daggers drain all strength
This man has no business being here...

It's All Too Late

It's all too late, the chair, the bed
The half baked notions running round the head
The hasty appliance of preventative measures
picked and left, seemingly at leisure

It's all too late, the chance is gone
and now the inevitable, it won't be long
Blasé were they with the pills and assessments
weighing up well being against private
investments

It's all too late, for reassurance
about this test of unjust endurance
What has been done will have to suffice
as now, fate clamps down its deadly vice

It's all too late, for regrets and if only's
The forgotten have secrets known only to the
lonely
Now the time has passed for comforting lies
No more thwarting expectations or wiping tears
from dry eyes

Just days at a loss, quiet and in state
Now it is most certain, now it's all too late

The Prayer

Oh Tempest, oh Scorn, oh Glorious Power
Take not my heart, or my soul, this hour
But take thy mind, let it be at rest
Release this burden, this erroneous test
Free this Warden, this Keeper of Old
Freeze this warmth, boil this cold

Oh Tempest, oh Threat, oh Radiant Noon
See here these threads for you to consume
Do not be tempted by such other things
As love or grief or all else they bring
Or integrity or courage, leave such things be
Gladly I'll wrestle such notions eternally

Oh Tempest, oh Judge, oh Deadly Flower
Does it not please, how I beg, how I cower
Plead and bequest for your endless mercy
Bleeding with regret for the failings I see
If only such sights didn't extend so far
Shining brightly, in the morn, as the Morning
Star

Oh Tempest, oh Scourge, oh Limitless Vision,
Do what you will, yours is Holy permission
I only utter this as a show of acceptance

To how I perceive thy wondrous presence
In all that's struck, hammered and nailed
Lost and won, strengthened and failed

Oh Tempest, oh Scion, oh Husband of Nature
I fear all is just a bet, some grandiose wager
For stories of Job play fetch with my peace
As notions of Justice won't barter release
No rest can be seen, no horizon in sight
The fight is fought lost, to the petulant night

Oh Tempest, oh Breaker, oh Irresistible Force
I surrender my helm, my compass, my course
Not one to care for fortune or fame
With survival alone long being the lone flame
Burning fiercely bright in the ancestral gutter
Now, even such light begins to splutter

And I too with it, so it would seem
Recalling forgotten and never had dreams
While trapped in this still-thickening skin
That seeks to keep out what I long to let in
Oh Tempest, oh Maker, oh Highest Ascent
Take it all, it's done, and utterly spent

What's He Listening To? II

Jake and Ana excitedly threatening
to take your momma out all night,
show her what it's all about

Kazu angrily lamenting
she doesn't understand this at all
these are uncertain feelings

Jose climactically commanding
we'll weaken what they say
by how we love

Arvo painfully orchestrating
the distance felt from Alina
the silence growing

Beth ethereally pleading
that we have a war to fight
but how can it feel so wrong

Dan decidedly chanting
about wanting to go deeper
but not being so brave

Maynard capriciously contending

that life will have its way
so just enjoy the ride

Tom ruinously admitting
that you're all I need
keep breathing

Neal riotously prophecising
that someday love will find you
just break those binding chains

Bill solemnly expressing
how he left his mother
and his sisters too

Sebastian achingly realising
Je sais, l'amour naissant
Je rêvais, pourtant

Music is so important
without it, I'd be lost
It soothes the raging currents
and thaws the ancient frost

Whether one wants to dance
or dwell in uncertain thought
Music provides the essence
as the bean does to the coffee pot

It's the kindling to the necessary fire
the foundation of the life saving road
Music will always pave the way
to a more fulfilled and rested abode

Trapitalisim

This has always been the way
of the cosmic ebb and flow
Everything still yet to come
must come yet still to go

Everything is give and take
unless you're found in need
so dumbing down my sense and heart
I surrendered to lust and greed

An open admission of salient guilt
that crept up one blackened night
That sense, newly ignited, firing steam
The revelation plainly in sight

Always trying to fit myself in
where the fits were bent and warped
Changing the meaning of kin
Playing on swamp laden courts

A game predetermined
by a stonewalled vagrant lot
where the rules are ever changing
and the breakers are quickly shot
where the ground has been deep treated

with a specialised ill coating
that conspires to shred and break ankles
and rises to stab those found floating
while those multitudes of sorrowful eyes
that stare painfully as you fall
apathetically turn away
deaf to your pleas and calls

That isn't to say there's no enjoyment
in having the odds so highly stacked
but it's a poor use of inner strength
and celebrates what one lacks

There are no teachings here
in how to live, build and fortify
Only a blitzkrieg of dire lessons
on How Best Not To Die

Pictures

Baubled lights pulse rhythmically around you
You pose gleefully, warming the cold evening
air
Your blue woollen hat, white winter coat, and
fluffed white scarf blend perfectly into the
winter scene
You time it so, that as you raise your hands, the
lights glow brighter; clearly a demonstration of
your power!
Joyful silly laughter rings out like Christmas
bells, as you commit wholehearted to the bit
I take a few pictures and combine them into a
short animation
The slideshow does well to showcase your
talent, but still falls far short of the real thing

Pictures always do

Such snaps snap us right back, applying more
rose-tint to each moment as the heart and body
double down in their longing

It's easy to get lost in it
Easier then to turn bitter towards the barren
horizon that extends in all directions

giving promise of a vagrant future

But that's dire talk, spoken by fear, fear and all
his brethren, a sickly commune who had their
part, nay their Starring Role
in how this World now looks .

So different from the scene in this picture
and yet, this is the reality that was born of it,
propagated by that which was already there

Such an important thing, to have this resource
this insight into the pattern
this lifeline from a beautiful past
that although may shatter the moment
gives promise of a glorious tomorrow

Answer

It's funny how time
makes fools of us
Always toeing the line
not wanting a fuss

Until suddenly the lens
goes out of focus
The diver gets bends
Hope becomes hopeless

It's easy to get caught up
in the flow of strife
To compromise and cut up
To blood the knife

With nothing more precious
than your own heartfelt dreams
Hanging now fleshless
and torn at the seams

But dreams are resilient
and can bare much pain
Those pronounced dead
will come to rise again

Again and again and evermore
they'll scrape, heave and crawl
crying out your blasted name
until you answer their desperate call

The Draw of Oblivion

There's nothing there
where the stars never formed
A vast and empty lot
with eternity, adorned

No particles of mass
to swirl and coalesce
No figments or ideas
to argue for what's best

No categories to class
or lovers to underdress

Just a vacuumus region
Stagnantly cold
Where nothing is born
and nothing grows old

Where love has never blossomed
and hate has never grown
Where joy has never touched
and despair's never known

Where purpose has never visited
and grief has no home

There, dreams have never been dashed
and hope has never been sundered
Words have never caused harm
and hearts have never been plundered

At times in our lives
we may long for such a place
where history never started
and humans never raced

When all seems determined
in conspiring to burden
you know where the faults lie
but you can't get a word in

You try to speak up
and the vibe soon turns sinister
threatening disease
with no cure to administer

And each sleepless night
you let yourself dream
of being there
of being nothing, serene

But everything that IS
must eventually come to pass
The joy of content nothingness

can never truly last

Even the hardest times of all
that span forever and an age
will themselves turn tail and run
as change itself turns the page

We may feel forever more laden
and evermore know only the fray
but against the draw of Oblivion
we must fight for a better day

Signs

An overheard phrase in a nearby conversation
A nostalgic song playing over a tinny
marketplace tannoy
A graffiti'd wall

It's nearly impossible
to describe

Rationality struggles
in the face of something
so significantly small

Then again, how rational are the stars?
How logical, life?

Cosmic Entities dance Carousel
beyond the void
to the rhythm
of timelessness
while
sub-atomic surfs of force and will
coincide
and collide
in instant obliteration

and here we are in the middle

waiting patiently for that loving moment
that as it comes, passes by without a nod

here we are in the middle

conspiring ruinously for that confrontation
that as it rises, simply evaporates

How exponential, this Chaos
How far beyond understanding, this Law

Yet how reassuring it is to know
that despite the intricacies of the infinite
the Cosmos still orchestrates harmoniously
to show all who have belief in vision

that they aren't alone
that the path is true
and to not give up

Start of the War

You know where the spikes lay
rusted and impatient
seeking blood
You know when the blade drops
in silent reverence
cutting through the atmosphere
You know how the waters boil
flowing untethered
consuming all

Most would say that's 'half the battle'
for whatever else is in store
but such a sentiment, to me, unravels
for I know, it's the start of the war

You know where the joy is found
to appreciate it
yet it is avoided
You know when the times has come
to take your leave
yet you linger
You know how the fear grows
as dusk approaches
yet it's welcomed

Such forethought presents a clear choice
aspirations to hold or ignore
It's a difficult thing to come to terms with
An infantry position, at the start of the war

You know where the sleeper resides
patiently waiting
for chaos to call
You know when the past clings
demanding attention
to let it tire
You know how the scales unbalance
spilling dreams
It's nothing personal

Yet an old gnawing sense persists
like gentle waves upon the shore
It's too late to take up arms in defiance
it's too late for the start of the war

But do we turn traitor to our own alliance?
Stand ever restless sick to our core?
Become a glazed slave to each new appliance
that seeks to replace our wisdom and lore?
Upon the unnatural we've grown too reliant
to an exponential chorus we implore
A chorus demanding complete compliance
demanding an end to the start of the war

You know where the tripwire lies
longing for company
in release
You know when the trigger strains
building bloodlust
to ease it off
You know how the bomb primes
in gleeful haste
Just breathe

The battle has been long fought
and half may again be in store
but each victory will be for naught
unless you surrender, to the start of the war

The Man

The man, the man tells you how shit you are
while still expecting your help
He'll use all kinds of tactics, he'll growl, he'll
bark, he'll yelp
He'll get you young, and ensure you know, how
difficult it will be
with venomous tongue, and rusty hoe, he'll plow
thy field for thee
He'll make you think that he knows best while
salting all the land
He'll make you drink from sour wells sieved
through dirty sand
He'll make you feel like a grand mistake,
forsaken by the gods
and laugh and joke as you're about to break

The man will take the things that are held closest
to the heart
He'll hold them high above you and say that in
them, you have no part
Not meant for you are such things of privilege,
wrong are support and understanding
In this furnace fire all that matters, is how long
you can hold your hand in

In this he will bend over backwards to help, he'll
even hold your elbow
and cry aloud right there with you, grimly
savouring the show
Once satisfied he'll loosen his grip, and profess
that you're ok
as from your blackened hand the flesh drips

The man has much to teach, for all who can bear
to take the lesson
to see through the bitter eyes of regret and pain
and loss and aggression
to understand that the man has faced and lived
such things as well
and now passes on, only what he knows,
knowing only of going through Hell
The aim is not to excuse the willful disregard,
disgust and torment
but to know that same framework lies within,
beyond excavation, abhorrent
yet still can be built upon to serve grand purpose
given the right architectural input

There is nothing that can't be overcome
there are plenty of solutions
there is no reason that can be given
for not cleaning up your own pollution

It's Not Your Voice

Its not your voice
You know that
It comes from elsewhere

Discerning its source
depends on understanding its intention

Does this voice push you on
or pull you back?

Raise you up to challenge the heavens
or persuade you down to stay in line?

Does it soothe you? Or does it blame?

Be mindful

for the Voice of Reason can be devilish
the Voice of Ambition Holy
depending upon the circumstance

Be mindful

and remember

it's not your voice

2am

I dreamt your arms were reaching
jonesing to hold me tight
then awoke the silent blackness
of the stale and lonely night

The strength of such deep longing
almost too much to bare
in these times of rampant solitude
there is little strength to spare

Yet somehow there is comfort
among these ruminations
Memories of the kind of love
that gives meaning to Creation

But alas, therein lies the fault
one replete with terrible cost
to base reality upon your love
is to be forever lost

I loved you far too greedily
inevitably, did it sour
a taste that is much sweeter still
than this ungodly bitter hour

Transmogrification

What do you make of this?
This time, this state
Not like when and where it used to be
and not yet here or there or in company
but still to come and be dwelled upon
before itself passes by
true as night becomes dawn

Of this we have
practically no control
it's best to assess
what you don't think you know
but it's left to the side
as we settle on down
living like Kings
with our paper-thin crowns
until life conspires
to test their mettle
kicks up dry dust
that will never settle
gives two options
both quite unfortunate
demanding a price
that's truly extortionate

The first is to adapt
to change and overcome
to leave who you were behind
in the shadow of the sun

The second is to break
to spiral and withdraw
to lay down and present your neck
to life's cruel, gnashing jaw

The choice seems obvious
to the outsider
but so does the trap
of the web of the spider
It's not until you find
yourself being the fly
that you realise both
are just different ways

to die

Fool

I saw it coming
flirted with its insinuations
I watched
as the flame died
and now
I sit in the memory
of its warmth
cradling the cold, wet, ash
of what was once
your most loving embers

If Only

If only I could just get back
to who I was before
the weeds took root
in my memory stores

I'd tear myself away
and the whole world asunder
I'd carve out a terrible path
and rise up from under

Twisting forks
Spinning knives
Taking names
Outing lies
I'd strike out against
any who would say
that all there is
to this world is dismay

For all that swirls and lurks in the dark
is all that shines and radiates in our hearts
is all that rolls and punctures and splits
is all that splinters and hawks and spits
is all that hugs and loves and sits

Patiently

waiting for the tears to stop
waiting for the tide to turn
waiting for the penny to drop
realising, you can never return

Still, on it goes, amidst the chaos

If only I could just get back

If only I could just get back

In Meditation

Splintered
in a gracious cell

One stands
at the window to eternity
and weeps

While the Other
stares balefully
upon the foreign scene

The Journey

I walked into the Eldrich fire
and burnt you from my skin
but the scars, they solemnly ache for you
and condemn me for my sin

They glow with renewal in the night
and reject all calming balms
I sit and etchedly stare at them
with boiling brow on frozen palms

I sat among the Tigers Pride
with aim to let it be consumed
I looked the King right in the eye
but he only understood

He raised his claw and bared his teeth
I prepared myself for the rend
but then he moved to comfort me
promising that this wasn't the end

I sought out the Words of the Wise Men
hoping they would take your place
that their ways would sway my awareness
and their insights fill your space

But their lessons were pale and fraught with
holes
in regards to the bondage of our hearts
though I must admit, their teachings helpful
in living on, apart

I called you as the sun burnt high
We spoke in tongues for hours
and from the salted dirt and clay
sprang green leafstalks and vibrant flowers

With speed they grew in glad response
to the warmth and colour of your voice
a nourishingly sweet tonality
that left them no other choice

Some grew in hope of future threads
of rekindling romance
and soon their message began to spread
taking on a fighting stance

They seek to bask in your radiance
and only ever drink in your light
They'll never get their fill of you
or care to make things right

They want to keep you close to me
so that they may freely feed
I understand their nature

I feel their withdrawn greed

I turned my back to their chorus
of reasoning and regret
I focused on the joy of love
that has no cage, bars or net

We wrap up softly, and in reverence
with pleasantries and silly jokes
while the pleading nettles and sharpened vines
grow to threaten and bind and choke

Great Tendrils swarm, but are driven back
with machinations built of my throne
and bloodied scythes of yesteryear's love
that turns hearts wants to stone

I'll not have them take from you
and I'll not have them return
If upon this crop my love depends
then all of it must burn

If among this crop my heart I find
then ash is to be its fate
for I'd sooner die by honourable flame
than live such a burdenous state

I'd sooner fade into nothingness
with these companions of regret and pain

and hold them to me forever
than risk harming you again

I found myself in white wilderness
amid crumbled ruin and waste
and kneeling firm upon the arid plains
I thanked God for your patience and grace

For your insight, your love
your boundaries and strength
For your joy, your hope and your care

Then I began the journey on
as a fresh lily scent
filled the air

Easy Now Mate

Here, easy now mate
There's no need to go so far back
The past is what it is, there's no mistake
but you're letting it kick ya in the sack

Like, Jesus Christ man, don't let the devil win
All this doom and woe-ish self-heresay
What you focus on is what you become
You know? It's a self-fulfilling prophecy

I know grief needs it's time to be
but it can't be carried round past it's due
otherwise it'll poison all else that comes
like, mate, c'mon, look what it's done to you

And it's not grief alone, I know of the rest
I know how deeply it goes
but you're shrivelling up man, I can't stand by
You've got what it takes to grow

You've got what it takes to break on through
to contest, to prosper, to evolve
You've got all the tools inherently
You've got the strength, the will and resolve

So here, take it easy now mate
good times are always getting nearer
and if you're looking for a reason
why any of it's worthwhile
just have a look in the mirror